The Faces of Galle Face Green

poems by

Suwanda Sugunasiri

TSAR
Toronto
Oxford
1995

The publishers acknowledge generous assistance from
The Ontario Arts Council and the Canada Council.

Photograph on front cover by Hubert de Santana.

Author photograph by Mo Simpson.

Canadian Cataloguing in Publication Data

Sugunasiri, Suwanda, H.J.
    The faces of Galle Face Green

Poems.
ISBN 0-920661-52-1

1. Sri Lanka - Poetry.   I. Title.

PS8587.U48F3   1995   C811'.54   C95-932509-3
PR9199.3.S84F3   1995

Printed and bound in Canada

TSAR publications
P. O. Box 6996, Station A
Toronto, Ontario M5W 1X7
Canada

Other Works by Suwanda Sugunasiri:

Yamayaudde (Life Struggle), 1962 (short fiction, in Sinhala)
Meeharak (Idiots), 1964 (short fiction, in Sinhala)
Sri Lankan Literature (special issue of *The Toronto South Asian Review*, 3.2), co-edited with A V Suraweera, 1983
The Literature of Canadians of South Asian Origins: An Overview and Preliminary Bibliography, The Centre for South Asian Studies, University of Toronto, and The Multicultural History Society of Ontario, 1987
The Whistling Thorn: An Anthology of South Asian Canadian Fiction, Mosaic Press, 1984

For Swarna
for 32 years of caring and love

CONTENTS

And Other . . .

An Introductory Word

It's a pity nobody forewarned me that going overseas would be hazardous to my creative health! And it's interesting, or should I say "enlightening," to use that overworked gem, how both comfort and discomfort should be a creativity-killer. (Didn't the Buddha eschew both extremes, of indulgence and self-mortification, in his successful search for "spiritual creativity," i.e. Enlightenment?) The comfort was the all-expense-paid Fulbright scholarship to the US for academic study. And the three years of classes, assignments, library and raw survival was enough to kill me, never mind my creativity!

But life in Canada, after the initial period of two (and sometimes three!) jobs a day, gave me all the time in the world (and enough money), but you only had to be a non-mainstream Canadian (no "visible minorities" in the days of yore!) to have experienced the cultural hostility during those early sixties that sucked out whatever creativity that was left in ya! The best artistic ability I could garner was to produce a popular *Sinhalese* play, *Nari Bena* "Jackalson-in-law." To be selected to perform at the St Lawrence Theatre in downtown Toronto, as one of the ten best "Heritage Language" plays of the year (1980), was indeed gratifying. Taking Toronto's Harbourfront by storm with a Sinhalese Low Country Dance—well, you could take that as an egotistic exaggeration of a performance given as part of a Sri Lankan dance repertoire at Canada's 125th centenary, but it helped to keep my creative adrenaline going. But I must have been angry enough to write, in 1987, the piece "Step Down Shakespeare, the Stone Angel is Here" (*Multicultural Education Journal*, 5.2, 1987)—arguing for the recognition of *Canadian* literature, and for the expansion of the definition of "Canadian literature" to mean,

> the literature written by writers of any ethnocultural origin, who were born in Canada or elsewhere but are presently living in Canada as a citizen, landed immigrant or resident, and whose writing is in English, French, a Native language or another heritage language, about the content, theme or setting in Canada or elsewhere, and is primarily, but not exclusively, intended for a Canadian audience, reflecting a sensibility that can be best described as a "Canadianizing world culture."

Today I can write an obituary to my plea, in the gratifying knowledge that the Canadian literati has arrived at precisely such an understanding. I take humble pride in that perhaps my report to the Secretary of State, *The Literature of Canadians of South Asian Origins*, along with others under the same project on other cultural groups, might have played a role.

But that same struggle through the cultural slush, though, must have rekindled my creativity, for after twenty dormant years following my second collection of short fiction (in Sinhala), I was writing, to my surprise, poetry, and in the English medium! "Disarming Death" in this collection, on my way to Sri Lanka for my father's funeral, was the first product. Since then, amidst my academic teaching and writing, community involvement in and media appearances on multiculturalism, Canadian Buddhism and interfaith relations, writing for the *Toronto Star* and the occasional piece for the *Globe and Mail*, my creativity, essentially poetic, has been sporadic. Which explains the spread in years of the poems that appear in this collection. As the cities associated with the poems indicate, travel seems to have been a creativity generator, too! The sub-headings—"Women," "Politics" and "Buddhism"— pretty much show where my head has been during these years.

As I present these poems to you, for your enjoyment or close critical scrutiny, I close with some acknowledgements. "Bridges" and "Women on Tape" first appeared in the *Toronto South Asian Review* (3.2 and 4.3 respectively), the latter also appearing in Diane McGifford's *The Geography of Voice*. I thank Pat Weldon for her comments on some of the poems, and the Ontario Arts Council for its partial financial support during the editing of the collection. (The photo in the cover comes thanks to the ever-obliging Hubert de Santana, artist, poet, fiction writer, and travel writer for the *Globe and Mail*.) Finally, it is with respect I acknowledge the helping hand of Nurjehan Aziz, the smiling face, the gentle heart and the creative mind behind the business successes of TSAR Publications.

Suwanda Sugunasiri
September 9, 1995.

Of Women . . .

PROMISCUITY

Sheik angered by shoplifting charge:
two wives, daughters, lady-in-waiting convicted.
—*Daily Telegraph*, London, August 28, 1985

Pinched us he,
our Sheik, our dolly cheeks,
Your Lordship,
as we were
dispatched, covered
head to foot.

The Boulevards of Paradise
in our palms, how
boring the
crossing, petrodollars
flowing in one direction
perfumes diamonds in the other!

Only one of each I
had, my sister-wife five,
every item in
stock in our rat hole!
The girls it was, y'see,
who went to town,
like us
low V-neck mini
their hot number.
The lady-in-waiting had a
mere Calvin Klein
panty and bikini top,

when
the private eyes
swooped

Your Lordship, we pray,
do give us this day.

3

The fine we shall not pay!

We love those bars
to gaze at the stars
to heal our scars.
Do let
the bard
in us
release won in
prison bra-less
panty-less, strumming
a song
of promiscuity
cool air our
betrothed

(1985, London, England)

WOMEN ON TAPE

To Malini

Side la. *Chair in the Corner*

1.
On her second shift
in the small kitchen as I walk in . . .

"Sorry I couldn't
meet you at Gatwick . . .But
really
I love it
believe me
every minute of it
back from work.
Even polish
the silver and brass
and
back again.

"Energy I'd say
energy,
that's what.

Guess I've been brought up that way!"

2.
"Has it been
honestly, a week, since we left London driving through
Paris and Monte Carlo and Rome . . . ?"

The night out
in Venice   the dinner
at Rio Grande   the wandering minstrels
the wine
the lulling train ride . . .

"You're my brother.
Like one at least.
He's a good man, this
my man
your buddy.

"But . . .
but how long I mean
tell me
can I be
as but a chair
in the corner?"

3.
"Great to be back
in my wonderful
kitchen!

" 'I'm sick
of cooking'? Oh,
words on a wallplate! Just
a joke. Reminds
me to love
cooking.

4.
"This my man
a good man . . ."

(1985, London, England)

Side 1b. *Wives of London*

She came
to bid us goodbye
out of the house
down the stairs
("elevators bore me")

thrilled at each step
exuberance decorating
the face.

Yesterday she
served us a scrumptious meal.
"Cooked
all day," her husband said with
a mocking pompous grin
"Not
all day," she protests.

"Yesterday he
lunched with the Israeli ambassador, tomorrow
off to Hawaii. The UN
pays him but not
me.
Would be interesting to play
cards with him; beat me
all the time
way back when.

"I unstitch and stitch
my jackets skirts
to fit myself in,
add lace brocade colour,
look in the mirror
lipstick rouge
pummelling the face.

"Just look at that
water, how beautiful, meandering
down the street
into the drain.
Have you this scene in Toronto?

"I can
take the Metro, you know,
from one end

to the other.
He
does the driving
carefully
calculating.

"Tonight Jakarta
stopover with his folks en route, who knows!
Perhaps a swim a sip
of the local arrack under the fan."

"Come again,"
she says, waving
smiling
the wet tear over the lined face
brown of long years,
the wife of London Paris Geneva Tokyo.

(1985, Paris)

Side 2a. *Guardians and Angels*

Skiing
I go on TV
sun I bathe
by the window. The
little ones' messing
falling laughing
make my day. The ocean
of German around me too much
to fathom, cross,
he navigates
with so much ease,
the four walls my guardian
he
my angel.

(1985, Vienna)

Side 2b. *Song of Femininity*

In an Egyptian mummy-coffin
DuMourier Players
deep in eternal slumber beside
a wine cellar rotting
inside out
the smell enough
to kill the dead
scotch vodka gin strewn in splinters
of glass, the outer shell
plastered with Playboy Penthouse
centrefolds dissipating
at the touch.

The lotus
lilting by
above the slime
in peacock plumes
the maxis midis
crushing under the draped sari, beckoning
the nymph mother lover
in me, strutting
to a minuet
stringing a song
of femininity on a
sitar.

The woman I am
released
from bondage.

(1985, Toronto)

LIVIN' W'M'N

walking
    the mile under the weight of the hoe
splashing
    a smile at the customs desk
keeping
    the records through the factory din—

        the woman
        in china,

owning
    taxis signing cheques
feeding
    hungry tanks at the gas bar
hustling
    the mechanics on intercom—

        the woman
        in austria,

womanning
    men's toilets glum glued to the face
swiveling
    on a chair for visitor queries
directing
    the traffic at the central square—

        the woman
        in yugoslavia,

elfing
    the best silks in Spadina's backlanes
cleaning
    the floors beating the night streets
wrapping
    bologna at the Kensington market -

the chinese
black
portuguese
white
woman of toronto,

nipping
no bud before it grows
allowing
their men to sip scotch at home
looking
away as kids run amok
inviting
governments to turn a blind eye,

w o m e n
l i v i n'
the
best
they can.

(1985, Toronto)

AT THE SHREDDER

I
"You don't want to be
Victorian. A
little
shoulder
can't
do no harm,
babe."

The freedom
away from home
in Hollywood too dear
a bird to
let go of, you
uncovered
your shoulder,
thread
at a time, barely
glancing,
in obvious
shame, at the
Director
w o n d e r i n g
wondering if,
anyone
was withdrawing
their eyes, only
to see
the benign nod.

Taking you for a ride
in the sleek
Coupe de Ville
of the fatherly smile
you were
reminded: "not
many men

return from the
war."

Imaging the wrath
of dying a maid,
in innocent
competition you
let your neckline
drop (told
the English nobility does it, too),
crying
a polite smile when
eyes coveted
on the compressed
flesh
vying
to escape.

"Try it on, you'll
get to like it, if not
now . . .You know
What I mean . . .
The music, the glitter
helps but I
make my
money
on your shapely
legs."

With each applause
led by
men
you, conscripting
the coquetish step,
flirting
changing partners
maxi midi mini.

II

Resting your job
on the Executive lap
away from the envious eye,
you projected
a wider screen, willing
your modesty
to the care of
the bodice the pantyhose.

In redemption
for competing
for the honour
to bare the most
of you on the beach,
raking in a mound,
you were offered
freedom
of the
flesh,
designer ads keeping
an iron watch.

Scuffling over
one another
at the Eaton Centres,
you unveiled
in grateful benediction
your liberated
thighs
the exposé ending
at the fringe,
hair quivering
through,
the taut flimsy thread
screening
the reddening lips.

Champagne flowing
their yes-men bought up
more
stocks, and
not forgetting
to thank
paraded you
in expensive high heels
to the cheers
of onlookers,
your sex goddess
hoping
to catch the next train
to the
centrefold.

III
Your sisters hailed
your Right
to your Body,
perhaps not
telling you, as
the men
didn't either,
by whom
the plan was
designed executed,
you perhaps
not realizing, too,
how they had
got you
again
in measured step
to the jacuzzi whirlpool
of the yen
of shredded
morality.

                    (1986, Toronto)

15

MICE IN DUNCE CAP

To Karuni

I

Uncoiling,
one by one the mice
on their marks,
get set, their
extended antennae tapping
into the receding
thud
ready to sprint, out
of their cheese-filled
cage, bag
and baggage stacked
with holiday clothing. The
mother mouse
winks.

Brakes released,
Gold Card in hand,
she steps on the gas, the
helium-filled wheels
of the family Benz, gliding
like on a hot-balloon,
feelings on a
flying trapeze.

Winding down
the windows the
little ones breathe,
nostrils
cavorting
with the fresh smells,
the capless hair,
a ballet
in the wind.

II
Nibbling on the cheese
back
in the gliding cage
the mice the mother
play
the dunce-capped
as the cat
ambles in
through the tinsel
welcome
of the door ajar,
walking all over
its territory.

The face make up
oozing, the
slobbering tongue
osculates
limb by limb,
the spit
of self-compassion of bounden duty
cocooning
the bubbling throbs
in rigor mortis.

Well-hidden
under the bourgeoning clump
of the professional paw,
the red-hot claw-tips
char
the tender bodies
sometimes bleeding
sometimes numbing.

(1987, London, England)

17

Politics . . .

THE PULPING OF A MAPLE

Down the chute in gushing waters
the logs, cleansed
of guilt
down the elevator, shame sheared off
against tunnel walls,
squirm . . .
their little
maple leaf
bludgeoned through inferno,
the flat sheets in
laid to rest posture, moved
like cattle,
dis-
membered . . . and
twang
in steel wires, captivity
complete, receive
the metal
embrace,
"Made
in Canada."

The guide in white-
wash smile
serenades
through the din in familiar tune how
"we all
win" when
tender maple hands go
necking "the
softness
of the feather,
the strength
of a horse" in Made-in-Canada
boxes.

Pulp souvenir, wrapped

in stars and stripes
enlighten
us New Brunswick
to Ontario, the
final words,
"We're an
American
company!"

(1984, Fredricton)

TO A FISH VENDOR

As you slice, chop
facing away from me
the smell stampedes
my senses
to a 1550 AD, the red blood
of history
sparring
every fibre, how
you came in
shiploads for spices,
greeting us
with bullets if we
dared
resist
for a full
century and half.

You decorate
your face
with a smile,
proudly display
a *Toronto Star* cutting

how you
eke out a living
at your Kensington market,
surreptitiously hiding
the reverse page,
the wife-battering the child-killing
the drunken illiteracy—
the culture you brought
to civilize us.

Tell me I am wrong
as I visualize
you with gun in hand
cross fixed,
deliriously charging
like a horde
of northern caribou
in heat, though
page after page
tells me you did,
trampling underfoot
the pages of a
two-thousand years.

Your conquest
life
of our parties today,
our colonized minds
gyrating
to your *baila* dance tunes,
singing praise—darn it,
"Conquering land
descend Mara,
the Lord of Death
from
Lisbon"!

Why, fish vendor, why
did you steal

my peace? Are the
red-brick houses your
rows of hell-prison, the
fires of poverty, your
karmic outcome,
plunderer?

What the fake? What
the real? The
innocence
in your face   or the
cruelty
in your history?

The spice you
didn't take—
critical-compassion—all
I have
to help you bide by,
till
you snap out
out of your
karmic misery,
garnering merit
in mind body word, as
you alone can
in a new universe.

(1985, Toronto)

BRIDGES

I
Strange
    bedfellows
the cross, the hammer & sickle
Brahma-Vishnu-Siva
tied by language
loyalty gained
at gun point
striking terror
turning blind eye
                to aristocratic power
                upper-caste politics
                temple untouchability
uniting
against the common enemy
the hen that laid the golden egg
this common enemy
                the hand that fed
                nurtured cavorted
                through kings Elara, Raja Raja
                and Sri Wickrama Rajasingha.

The spoilt brats
in catholic anglican soviet palestinian american uniform
behind the Hindu smokescreen
into whose mouth
the pacifier thrust
at every cry
for more and more.

II

Remember?
these breasts you suckled
free education cradle to death
free health care   rice ration
ravenously

in mouthfuls
nourished the impoverished
barren land.

Remember too
as I opened my arms
let you hold on to me
as you struggled to walk
through generations
you crawled
and sprawled
all over me
happily for me
in Colombo hill capital Kandy
gem capital Ratnapura
from the cold climes of Badualla Nuwareliya
to the warm Hambantota
in small town Tangalla,
not just in Velvettithurai
and Mannar.

III
Now when in hunger
        for love
in crucified near-the-edge agony
I come,
your threat
turned blind eye blind ear
        to pleadings to stop
        the tyranny
reels out in my ear
your threat
made loud and clear
        in exploding bombs
        sophisticated arms
to cut me
at the very neck
from Jaffna to Hambantota
tying your roots

to other roots
                    beyond.
You say the blood of terror
is healthier
the milk of tolerance
of Dutugemunu Elara
phony.

Forget not
caught of guard
the master plan
the divide and rule
with their neocolonial GNP
bulging
each time
you raise your gun.

IV
Arunachalam, Ramanathan
co-freedom fighters
for one Lanka
these your models
not Chelvanayakam, Amirthalingam.
Read *Mahabharata, Ramayana*
Silappadikaran, Dhammapada
these your fountains
not *Das Kapital.*
Mao Castro Arafat
liberators all
but please
not ethnic enclaves
Ireland Cyprus Quebec.

Peace
never seen heard felt
your generation

cubs
cuddled by tigers
launched on the war path.

sharp claws
hurt
make deep scars.

Arjuna
urged by Lord Krishna
relented
"How can I fight my kith and kin."

Let the sandy beaches
the pearls the emeralds
the gentle breeze
the jobs you have
the land you own
the wealth you possess
all
lull you my wealth,
the children of the North,
out of your slavish slumber of
t e r r o r.

(1984,Toronto)

BETWEEN WORLDS

To Elizabeth
I
I could feel
the electricity running
down my arm
then . . .

as I sprung
a salute, parading
loyalty, my
uniformed ego
about to explode
into a firecracker
night, as you passed by
the sea of heads
flanked
by Brown Knights.

II
Today
in sovereign Canada
we

wait,
in multicultural splendour

rise,
as you enter
flanked by White Knights

stand
to attention,
to the tune
"God save the Queen."

My arm that saluted

suddenly
feels sore
to the very core.

Every gem every
thread you wear
anointed
with blood
of a million
upon millions whipped out
in your name
en-
snaring us
black brown yellow
with the promise, the
Heavenly Kingdom.

III
As you enter
as you depart
unaware
of the flutter
of the bird
in my heart,
you fling that charm
-ing smile, you alone
can summon
in such serene-dignity,
melting the
iceberg.

I salute you,
Enchanting
Lady!

(1984, Toronto)

ANOTHER LINK

All night long the
mother moos; I
look through the window.

The rest of the kine
awakened
by the rooster's call
graze around,
dressed
in black   comforting
the mother in
se-
pa-
ra-
tion, the
boulevard trees
showering
green shelter.

For the calf no more
the days of
umbilical milk,
the boulevard shade
traded
for the
corrugated roof.

The mother
tethered
udder manacled,
the machine-fed cask
bulges
with the milk
of life,
profit
gurgling
in the marketplace scuttle.

The mother
the calf
look on
in a graveyard silence
feeling
the frozen sham
in the farmer's
stroke.

Trees languishing,
one by one
the kine
in silent language
trade
the shade
for the burning pastures,
the farmer's footsteps a
distant memory
of another love
another link
shorn off
for cold profit.

(1985, On a Welsh farm)

THE FALL OF A CITADEL

"Helluva guy!" "Even
in death he
smiles," the
admirers said, marching
through the pages
of the visitor's book
in pressed suits.

The citadel of life
encircled, the
enemy advances,
dressed in
male mirth and mire
bottle after bottle filling
the moat,
the rounds of butt gunfire   clouding
the vision in
the chains of smoke,
with every
advancing year.

The army
penetrates. The
puff and the flow
too close
for comfort, the
defenders—the
arteries to the inner chambers—
in fatigues
collapse. The citadel
finally
conquered, the
frigid body lies   draped,
in a flag of
white suit—symbol
of surrender.

Tonight
in another household
camouflaged
in mirth and mire, the
enemy makes
the move   lining up
the armoury
of bottles and butts
until
yet another queen
in prime bloom
inherits
fond memories
of a warm body and
the handshake
of the mourners.

(1987, Toronto)

THE CONTEST

"Immigrant shot dead in midnight hold-up"— a Toronto news item.

Spare me
the torture—your
tears, my
body killed dead, my
daughter my wife, no
political whores, across
the nation's pages.

The cookbook legend how
violence there
led us here
only to face
another violence—what
a laugh!

You said this land was
free
of hunger oppression. Now
I know
the contest,
struggling
to keep from falling
asleep through
the darkest hours at
the gasbar milkstore
3:15 an hour perhaps 4:00,
running
four times as hard
still
divining no water
in the desert,
thorns
of racism sprouting
to receive every step,
wiser

by a hold-up bullet.

My will
to my wife my daughter—
"My death here,
your life there"!

(1985, Toronto)

HIROSHIMA

I am born
into another
samsaric station,
the heat
of
Hiroshima.

Could I not
melt
with them into the
warm arms
of the burning lava?

(1988, Tokyo)

THE KNIGHT AT THE SQUARE

(On a visit to China in 1972, the limousine in which the writer was travelling nearly collided with the only other limousine in the laneless but wide Tien Mien Square.)

See these peasants two-wheeling   their ware
adding their flair even at   the Square!
Army trucks cart along   the Red Army hordes
soldiers in tunic   holding on like toads

My trimmings and curtains   as at a ball
waltzing to my music at our   Tien Mien hall
stepping I vroom,   the armoured Knight
roaring to sixty,   yahoo, what a sight!
the soft touch, silk gloves,   the velvet cover
damned right you're,   the key to power!

The weight is right   the passenger a delight
ministers & queens   in their wealth and might
crossing blue oceans   flying by night
all in my power-chariot   sleek and white.

In laneless Tien Mien,   I race, I swerve
where I drive   my sole preserve.
These peasants on wheels, the baggies on trucks
why do they stare?   Their duty to serve.
Buttoned up in uniform   creased, well-pressed
My limo and me,   the Revolution at its best.

You, passenger dear,   under my good care,
the panic in your eye,   triggered from nowhere.
No damned rhyme,   indeed no reason.
Soon, I'm telling you,   it'd be high treason.
This, I remind you,   OUR very own Square.
Chairman Mao's   in the chair!

(1972, Beijing)

37

DOWN THE UPSTAIRS

To Yasmine

Had, has and will have
this language
illustrious
sons, pompous arrogant
when not
Machiavellian,

this language catapulted
across
lands and oceans,
the promissory note delivered
on an IMF silver platter,

castrating
the virility
of this other
of native soil, every
bud suckled
to its full bloom
on the smell
of rice of kasava,

in a tyranny of
disuse.

Shakespeare rides
on a palanquin,
the borrowed plumes
of profs and their
underlings
embellishing.

Wen-jen the Chinese literary man
Kalidasa in India, Murasaki in Japan,

the Sinhalese Wettewe composing
in sweat and tear,
wave
their flags of
pages
of honed antiquity,
barely avoiding
snarling stones.

Fencing
off a Churchill
chain of smoke puffed
in a European cold, Nehru
Sukarno Kenyatta Bandaranayaka stand
stand tall,
shoulder
to shoulder in
ceremonial dress,
invite
proudly
underlings profs whose memory
set in concrete
in the parrot chambers
of Laski Marx Ogden,
receiving
their only trophy,
mock jeer.

Tell me tell me
fairest of all,
which language indeed
does it all?

(1984, Toronto)

CRY OF THE GREAT BIRD

Plane carrying the country's most powerful crash in Africa
—news item

I
Stretched wings aerating the arid land
Moscow to Washington, the Great Bird glides
on to the tarmac, pride in its passengers teeming,
shrinking the world in half.

Huddled within panelled-oaks under the eagle eye,
the very best concur, signing out wars
setting on its way pigeons in a beeline.
That was forty-five.

II
Decorated for its role, wearing the decal
in the music of its humming wings the Great Bird
spirit away the best Ho Chi Minh City to Vatican City
shrinking the world by a half and half again.

Glasses lifted, burning the midnight oil
the best compliment, stare, eat up a thousand pads
but viewing in the table mirror their depleting heads
they dash to the Bird in search of solace.

III
Offering the load to the heavens in uproar
in homage, vibrrrrating in..to.. a trance
in a grand finale of a suicidal act
the Great Bird sheds its wings, dousing
the engine with tears wrenched off the think tank,
hiding in hot shame in a yellow, red blanket,
nosediving its anger in heated explosion
as it kisses the earth, renting
m i l e s   a p a r t heads and limbs
of the very best that failed!
                    (1988, Seoul, Korea)

THE FACES OF GALLE FACE GREEN

I. Innocence

On a visit
from a far away land
as I lay
eyes closed inviting
the sun's radiance,
I remembered
the faces
of Galle Face Green,

where
the grass scampered
with out little feet
frolicking past,

where the winds testing
our little hands
tugging at the string
with pirouetting kites
the waving streamers
teasing,

where a titilated promenade
rolling a welcoming mat,
the caressing spray
of the swaying waves,
the sensuous glow
of a waxing moon
courted
arms walking in arm
showering
loving glances.

II. Revolution

Oh yes I remembered, too,
with my heartbeat
galloping,
those other faces
of the grass the promenade the wind and the water
watching me
in awe
standing arm in arm
with a million others
on that May Day,
an excited worker bee
in a needled hive.

As if,
summoned by the
Guardian Dieties,
the seas
had come ashore roaring,
we poured in, wave
after human wave,

blue and red banners
choreographing,
to one tumultuous refrain—
"monk, healer, teacher
student farmer worker,"
the net
of camaraderie weaving
to the harmony, "Onward
socialist soldiers. . . "

the towering
Bandaranayaka we called Banda
leading,
the "Father of Socialism" Phillip,
N M Colvin the Trotskyite Twosome,
Communists Pieter and S A Wicks

flanking,
parading
the Parliament
of the Will o' the People,

unions marionetting
on the palms of
Mendis the Sinhalese
Shan (mugadasan) the Tamil
Thampo the Eurasian
Mohammed the Muslim,
vowing to uproot "forever"
Brown Sahib power,
drowning in the clamorous sea
the horse-riding Right-Honourables
the "go-slow-on-nationalism" Kotelawalas
the Yankee Dickie Jayawardhenas
the stomachache Dudley Senanayakas
all "capitalist pigs,"

pelting stones nearly
setting on fire
The Lake House, The Times
the Catholic the Tamil
mouthpieces
of a "decadent" past,

toppling
in one heave
the Sinhalese bus—
mudalali owners, the Indian
money-lending Chettiyars,
Cargills & Millers with their
luxury goodies,
the Shell barons converting
rupees to dollars,

we poured in,
I remember.

That was 'fifty-six when
streets danced
to the refrain
"Revolution
for ever."

III. Counterrevolution

A new wave dashed
on the cobbled wall
as I lay on the Green,
rubbing
the salt
in my eyes.

Now I heard
the new chorus in
many
voices:

1.
The hammer and sickle
thundered
through union halls,
the Galle Face Green
picking up the echo,
"Strike
while it's hot,
spineless Banda your target,
demand
down your tools."

"Long live N M Colvin
Pieter and SA back from the Kremlin"
the Fourth International applauded,
audience assured
of "the Undying Revolution."

2.
The choirs sang
in praise of the Lord.
Anglican Chelvanayagam,
Catholic Naganathan -
Tamil separatist fathers,
kissed their cross. . .
"Strike,"
you heard
them say,
the comrades.
"Sit-in.
Dangle
Gandhian respectability
use *satyagraha*, call it
'the grasp of truth,'
lie rest sleep
on the Green. Mail
your letters our pirate
couriers at your service,
til we get parity
of status
Tamil and Sinhala. Amen,"

"so,"
none heard them whisper,
containing the chuckle,
"we can continue
our quiet conversation
in English."

Laski days in the Motherland
foxtrotted
on Trostskyite faces.

The pulpits of the nation
new lease of life gained
buoyed the faithful:
"Nyet, Amen,

to the Socialist Devil, Amen,
vote
U(nited) N(ational) P(arty)
(of Uncles Nephews), Amen,
to speak English, Amen,
to send children
to Oxford Cambridge, Amen
import
cars cheese fashions, Amen,
provide work to
country bumpkins—
our
chauffeurs,
domestics, Amen Amen Amen!

3.
"Own we must,
shipping. . .
I mean, I
must,
Woman
in Cabinet,
first and only, thanks
Banda, but
people expect me
to show
my colour calibre
my Wijewardhena 'victory-builder'
legacy.

"Venerable Buddharakkhita 'the Buddha-protected'
king-maker
will not take
no
for an answer! Don't
be silly, child
(as they called each other),
don't believe them
the people

the sex scandals.
You know me—
Wimala 'the Pure One'—
can do no wrong, see
no wrong, in fact
our relations
strictly business."

IV. Tears

Hit
hard and true
he was
Solomon West Ridgeway Dias Bandaranayaka
as he lay
in an overflowing
pool
of red blood, the
Premier of the People
felled
by a bullet in his own
house
antiquated doors
pried open
inviting the fresh air
of his people.

Cooled
by tears
in an unending line
past jealous
temples churches union halls and presses,
crosses winked at sickles
business-suits-
in-Buddhist garb joining
in passing the gun
behind backs,
turning a nation's mourning
into a simple mantra,

"We lost a great son,"
stealing the thunder
of the masses.

V. Flight

As if
ears polluted by their
eulogies
even today
the Guardian Deities
rented their wrath
with tears of
torrential downpours,
the billowing waves
pounding and pounding
as if
to shatter
the rock-walled banks
that held the ground back
to devour
in one growling sweep
the Galle Face Green
where they
marched
sat
and sang
the wind howling in unison
"The Great Betrayal."

Drenched in the wet
of memory,
every blade of grass
cologning in its ear
a new eau de stench,
the sky
the promenade
turning sour,
my feet turned

north
shattering kites
to pieces
back to the distant land
kicking
the faces of the Galle Face Green.

(1982, Colombo)

THE ORCHID AND THE DOLLAR

I.
The petals
in anguish
as they
bleed,
the rustle of
the blue-gold mint
lulling
her into a
gnawing
tranquillity . . .

"Next, please,
next," she
entreats. . .
"the orchid
I've nurtured
through maiden years yours
while my senses
play dead."

II.
"Here, mother, take
it." She
hurls
them at her,
dollars
turned rupees,
earned
in the
tourist backlane.

III.
"Now to buy
the
day's
ration!"   (1982, Colombo)

Buddhism . . .

TO FLY AWAY

Cross-legged
he sits
smiling
hand in lap, under the
           d d d d
      o o o   h h h
    b b b bodhi i i i
    b b b   t   i i i
         r
         e
         e
     compassion
radiating
a "Come and see," wearing
the cross   kissing
the Torah singing
the Om   praising
Ahuramazda, my
Perfected *tapis d'orient*
rolls
out, receiving
your feet.

"Toss out
in noble abandon the
cross you
bear, walk
the Perfected Cool,
savouring
the Bodhi
shade
massaging neuron
calming the blue
flow.

"In retreat, shall we
not,

in single abandon let
go let go let go
in the wind   ~ ~ ~~~ ( ) ~~'~ ~ ---- ..
          ~~~~ ~' ~~ + '
          ~ ~ ~ ~~~~~~~ * ---- ...
          ~   ~~ ~~ ~~ #
          ~~~~~~~~~~~~~~ ///// ·········

the new label
bodhi label.

"Eyes unsealed
experience
the Full Awakening
name-
less
birthing
the seven smiles
buried within."

(1983, Toronto)

DISARMING DEATH

I myself not
see
in the dazzling
brilliance
of my breath-
    less consciousness,
your faint image
projected
on life's screen.

Moulded,
and masked,
by the living
in a Neanderthal seizure
with the clay
of a destruction siege,
go find your prey
in warm
bodies.

(1982, Schiphol Airport, Amsterdam)

Note: The desire (*tanha*) for destruction (*wibhawa*) is posited by the
Buddha to be one of three desires that keep one's cycle of rebirths
going.

WHAT-THERE-NEVER-WAS

I. *Blindness*

In life-preserving dement
we cement it in
in the tabula
of consciousness
at birth,

imaging
a mirage in it—
a "soul,"
goading
the ship deep-
er
into the
samsaric guagmire.

II. *Arrival*

Sitting
hour after hour after hour
leaving the ship,
the wise alone,
niche out
hair cracks,
sitting again
digging canals
through layer
through thick layer
of the muck of
ignorance.
Insighting
m a t
    t
   er
in its essential
flutter,

now born as   m t e
              a t r
the never-the -same-yet-
not-another* energy
cry die, to be
born again
across
the synaptic bridge,
the batting eyelid
light years behind,

the mind now

drained
of the oil
of the myth that fed,
hermetically sealed
allowing no return flow,

the gold
of the pan
of compassion
shining trough

on course
to Nibbana the
flame-free,

arrives

unearthing
a soul-there-never-was.
                (1992, Toronto)

Note: The Buddha explains that consciousness is never the same
from moment to moment, but because its flow is so fast that we see
continuity and permanence, giving it the label "soul."

THE VOW

Sizzling in the pan
sunny-side down, it
needless
my memory
to a kid-consciousness
when looking
in the eye
of the Compassionate One
I vowed
not to take
life

A vow lived for
twelve child years
broken
in twelve
pneumonia days,
my gnashing
conscience
soothed over
my mom's confident words,
"Quick source of protein, you
have to believe me,
son, un-
hatched, too."

Watching the charade
paraded
in a modernization float
on doctor's orders,
the Buddha
calligraphs
a face of
equanimity.

(1985, Toronto)

LIGHT IN A HURRICANE

(This poem avoids using finite verb forms, to reflect the Buddhist notion of action with no actor. The state of mind in the context of the poem *results* from the process of meditation itself.)

In green green green
the music waltzing,
now flaring up
in a rock n' roll amber
red,
along the floor
panel of my
AM-FM.

The conductor's baton
hyping the
violin's lust the
anger of cymbals,
the despot of the senses
shooting
its missiles
in-quick-succession
through my
mind.

Mask whisked off,
the recognition—
the pleasure cavern
writ large in green amber
and red,
the cross-legged sage
an intransigent rock
in a bullying
hurricane.

Mind-moments later
green to red in flight
the white monotone

of the mind's *taanpuraa*
cooling off the
panel.

(1987, Toronto)

PALACES

I.

Les palaises
   nt   mm   tu
  i   e   u   e   u   m
W   r S   r A   n
with roof
paintings
of a sistine chapel
well-laid gardens
arena
of warlords where
battle
plans are plotted
deciphering codes
in territorial ambition,
the Francis Josephs the Mings
Mara's Dance of Death
enticing
in a net of Greed
       Anger
       Ignorance.

II.

For Prince Siddharta,
the first battle won
conquering
the dancing seductress

sleeping naked salivating,
lavish meals, princely regalia
in *Ramya,* Winter
Palace the Beautiful
deciphering the code of
greed
ta-
ming
the Wolf
within.

The second secured over
economics of power, over
delirious victories over
kith and kin in
Suramya, le palais
extraordinaire of Summer
deciphering the code of
anger
taming
the Wild Boar within.

The third achieved,
the sick the old the dead
the homeless wanderer
in saffron
baring
the reality
hidden from view
by a loving
father,
wise men in stupor,
in *Subha,* the Autumn
Palace the Propitious,
deciphering the code of
ignorance
taming the Donkey within.
> (1985, upon recalling visit to Saheth Maheth (Savatthi), India ,
> where the Buddha spent 26 "Rains")

LORD, DISCRIMINATE

I.
Blacks, your
bosom buddies, you
gobble up on sight; the
Chinese you love
swallow in mouthfuls; the
whites your
soup-de-jour, you
lap up ravenously.

Fairminded
colour-blind
full circle you
come: blacks
your *soup-de-jour,* whites
bosom buddies . . .

II.
Across time
across land
you make
your rounds
poised
with the lethal needle
im-
permanence.

Amino acids
DNA cells
your elves,
clandestinely at work
from the very first
millisecond of
here-life,   uniting-
breaking up-uniting
draining
in a microscopic flux

the material-psychic
energy
frantically holding
the ground until
you arrive
to secrete
the final dose
terminating
here—life.

Your agents now
breathless
formless
within the flimsy walls—
the *bardo*—life
between life,
work
again,
with a glue
of *karmic* energy,
to revive
the hereafter
in changed
colour form.

III.
Anything
at all I'll
do, Lord
of Death.
Indeed anything—
support
apartheid
pray
five times a day if
you so decree, but
pray, don't tell me, Lord,
the truth
that life is

transient,
that the *samsara* lifecycle
is my
inheritance,
changing
colour shape, even
species.

Mercy I beseech, Lord.
Do discriminate! I
don't want to be a dog!
Allow me to pass
Hades   swim along
the Ganges   ascend
Mount Olympus
"soul" intact
in a suit of
one colour
the colour I
cherish now. Lord,
lavish your fairness
on them.

(1986, Toronto)

And Other . . .

THE OPERA

As I tread on the slippery ice
the villain zooms into my head,
spinning me around until it pulls
taut every neurone, clenching
its gutsy fist.

Walking the pages of life I met him—
or is it her?—dressed in suit
trim and proper with the facelift
of the sinister smile, the portfolio
well invested under its arm, ambling
the cushioned floor civilization has sewn,
making heads turn.

I watch my step lest it crack
the thin ice in the shenanigan.
Next I slide by many a solo
in the human desert where taut
neurons are dulled to the music
reverberating a mile.

Waiting
and waiting
for an applause,
the last hopes turn
into a remote wish,
each undernote
shattered
by a clenched fist
pounding.

Villain in command
on the slippery ice,
I step on the pound-
ed notes as I
rush
in dog   obedience.   (1988, Toronto)

PRISONER

Cloistered
in a two by two seat,

belted
across the chest

straight-jacketed
against the backrest

guarded
by passengers left and right

manacled
by floor luggage, legs sleeping

watched
by a Cyclopeon eye looming high

the sky-prisoner jet-sets
in mock comfort.

(1985, Calgary)

COMMUNICATION

rollingover to-oneside-now-to-another
in-unison in-foetal-position or-other
sealinglips closingeyes in-psychic-communication
nightafternight the lovers in years of
marital bliss.

(1985,Toronto)

COTTON RAIN

Hills and valleys
glisten
in the morning's bright
fleecing
an arctic blindness
in a silky sea
of cotton
layer upon layer,
the thin ones laying
bare a
hollowness of a closed canyon,
the sun making
its debut
"the star
of the intangible."

Descending
the fluffier worlds,
the sun still peering,
t h e t h i n   r a c e
thethick
far now
now near.
Psyching me out
through my window
the plane's fan
lilts, valley hill plateau
enveloped
in a cirrus nimbus . . .

Now below
the flat roof
like some overfilled
waterbed bag,
tottering
under the weight,
drip drip

as I walk
through customs
to my friend's
waiting car.

"What sun?" she asks.

(1987, Toronto)

WEDDING RINGS

To Swarna

Each malfunction
in the space shuttle
turned into a steel will
you lift off
guffawing into the sky
jettisoning the dead weight
fine-tuning
the precision instrument
of our life.

(1992, Toronto)

WATERPOEM

The wandering patches
staring
in my face a
history not read before
signing
on the dotted line
of real estate,
hammers
and shingles,
the plain face
of the brush strokes inside,
deface history,
saving face
claiming
victory.

Challenged
defiant thundergods
wait for the next moon
to sneak in
their best sharpshooters
through the fortified
shingles garrison,
the melted fury
finding a niche
in the skylight,
sending the household
for cover
of buckets and pots,
paper and rags.

A telephone call, and
the silicone
soldiers
called to duty,
thumb
their noses,

deflecting the anger
down the slope
through downpipe
claiming victory
again.

A week ago, in the living room,
victory robbed
by a lick on
my scalp,
watergods
now descending
camping
in the shower above,
transporting
in the secrecy
of the darkland
between joist and drywall
its armada
of water,
the sweat
of their copper tunics,
infiltrating
the drywall housing

I make
another call, and . . .

Sitting,
safe (?) again. . .
oh no, the well-
calculated cool,
drip. . .
sending me for cover. . .

Now I remembered
the soothsayer's word,
"Beware
of water"!   (1992, Toronto)